D0859772

GAYLORD F

TRAILBLAZERS OF THE WILD WEST

GUNFIGHTERS
OF THE WILD WEST

Jeff Savage

ENSLOW PUBLISHERS, INC.
44 Fadem Road   P.O. Box 38
Box 699   Aldershot
Springfield, N.J. 07081   Hants GU12 6BP
U.S.A.   U.K.

Library of Congress Cataloging-in-Publication Data

Savage, Jeff, 1961–
    Gunfighters of the Wild West / Jeff Savage.
        p. cm. — (Trailblazers of the Wild West)
    Includes bibliographical references (p.) and index.
    ISBN 0-89490-600-3
    1. Outlaws—West (U.S.)—History—Juvenile literature. 2. Peace officers—West
(U.S.)—History—Juvenile literature. 3. West (U.S.)— History—Juvenile literature.
[1. Robbers and outlaws—West (U.S.) 2. Peace officers—West (U.S.) 3. West
(U.S.)—History.] I. Title. II. Series.
F596.S2354 1995
364.1'092'278—dc20   94-33360
                                                              CIP
                                                              AC

Printed in the United States of America

10 9 8 7 6 5 4 3 2 1

Illustration Credits: Arizona Historical Society Library, pp. 7, 34; Denver
Public Library, Western History Department, pp. 4, 9, 23, 26, 27, 41; The
Kansas State Historical Society, pp. 14, 22, 29, 38; Courtesy Mercaldo
Archives, p. 42; Kristin McCarthy, p. 13; Nebraska State Historical Society,
p. 31; Western History Collections, University of Oklahoma Library, pp. 17,
20, 37.

Cover Illustration: Paul Daly

❦ CONTENTS ❦

The Earp brothers: Virgil (top), Morgan (left), and Wyatt (right).

1

THE O.K. CORRAL

The four notorious men walked slowly down Fourth Street. They were dressed in black. Each was carrying a gun. They were Doc Holliday and the Earp brothers—Wyatt, Morgan, and Virgil. They were out for blood.

Around the corner, on Fremont Street, four other men were waiting for them. They were the Clanton brothers and the McLaury brothers. They also had guns. It looked like terrible trouble.

It was a cold, blustery day in Tombstone, Arizona, on October 26, 1881. Ike and Billy Clanton, with Tom and Frank McLaury, had ridden horses into town to drink in the saloons. Virgil Earp was the city marshal of Tombstone, and he and his brothers didn't care much for rowdy cowboys like the Clantons and the McLaurys. Morgan Earp didn't appreciate it a month earlier when

Frank McLaury challenged him to step into the middle of the street to fight. Five months before that Wyatt Earp caught Billy Clanton in the saddle of his stolen horse. Each time, the Earps could have fought. Instead, they kept their cool.

It would be different this time. Ike Clanton, who did most of his fighting with his mouth, was drinking shots of whiskey in the Alhambra Saloon. He hated the Earps, and he claimed that Tombstone would be a better town without the brothers in it. Doc Holliday, a friend of the Earps, overheard Ike's boasting. Doc swore at Ike, then challenged him to a shooting match. Ike backed down.

Virgil Earp's responsibility as city marshal was to keep the peace; Wyatt and Morgan served as his assistants. When Virgil heard that Ike Clanton was threatening the Earps, he went out to find him. Virgil spotted Ike in an alley, approached him from behind, and grabbed his rifle. Ike tried to draw his six-shooter, but Virgil hit him over the head with a revolver. Then he arrested Ike for carrying guns within city limits.

Ike was wiping blood from his head when Wyatt Earp found him outside the courthouse a short time later. "You've threatened my life two or three times," Wyatt said. "I want this thing stopped."

Ike muttered a few words.

"You . . . dirty cow thief," Wyatt said. "If you're anxious to fight, I'll meet you."

The O.K. Corral was located on Allen Street in Tombstone, Arizona. The shoot-out occurred a block away on Fremont Street.

"I'll see you after I get through here," Ike answered, as he stepped into the courthouse.[1]

Later that day, Cochise County Sheriff John Behan was getting a shave in a barbershop when he noticed a crowd gathering on the corner. The barber said it looked like trouble, and Sheriff Behan hurried outside.

The Earp brothers were marching down Fourth Street. Because he was the marshal, it was Virgil's duty to disarm the cowboys. Sheriff Behan was a friend of the cowboys, mostly because he needed cowboy votes to be reelected sheriff. Sheriff Behan asked the Earps to hold on a minute. The sheriff said he would get the Clantons and McLaurys to give up their guns. The Earps agreed to wait. Sheriff Behan disappeared around the corner.

The Clantons and McLaurys were huddled around the corner on Fremont Street. Billy Clanton, Ike's little brother, didn't want to fight in the first place. He was mad at Ike for being such a loudmouth, but he had to stand beside his brother.

"Boys, you must give me your arms," Sheriff Behan said.[2]

The Clantons and McLaurys refused. The Earps resumed their march. Doc Holliday ran up from behind. The Earps were his best friends; he insisted on helping. Virgil accepted Doc's help. He deputized Doc right there in the street. Then Virgil handed Doc a shotgun.

Holliday and the Earps turned the corner. They peered down Fremont Street, and spotted the Clantons and McLaurys on the sidewalk next to the O.K. Corral. Sheriff Behan came running up to Virgil. He pleaded with Virgil not to go down there. The Earps didn't listen. They headed toward the cowboys.

A crowd looked on as Doc Holliday and the Earps reached the Clantons and McLaurys. The two groups stood less than ten feet apart. They stared each other down. The silence was broken with a *click, click,* as Billy Clanton and Frank McLaury cocked their six-shooters.

Somebody yelled, and the shootout began.

After the first shot was fired, Ike Clanton tossed away his pistol and ran up to Wyatt Earp. Ike begged Wyatt not to shoot him. Wyatt told Ike to fight or clear out. Ike ran away down the street.

Wyatt pulled a six-shooter out of his coat pocket, and shot Frank McLaury in the stomach. Frank hunched over, and stumbled into the street. Billy Clanton aimed his pistol at Wyatt, but before he could shoot, Morgan Earp fired a bullet through Billy's chest. Earp shot Billy again, in the wrist and stomach. Billy slumped to the ground.

Tom McLaury had been hiding behind a horse, but the horse bolted into the street. Doc Holliday took aim with the shotgun, and blasted buckshot into Tom's right side. Tom staggered down Fremont Street to the corner where he collapsed, dead.

Virgil Earp had not fired a shot. Suddenly, he felt a bullet tear into his leg. Billy Clanton was on the ground,

In less than one minute, the shootout was over. The victims, the McLaury brothers and Billy Clanton, were displayed in caskets under the sign "MURDERED IN THE STREETS OF TOMBSTONE."

bleeding but still shooting. Billy fired again, and this time a bullet ripped into Morgan Earp's shoulder. Morgan and Wyatt turned toward Billy and shot together—and Billy was dead.

Frank McLaury clutched his stomach and fired once more from the street. The shot struck Doc Holliday's holster, then grazed his side. Morgan Earp took aim and he shot Frank just below the right ear.

The shoot-out was over. It had lasted less than a minute. Three men were dead, and three more were wounded. The three dead cowboys were displayed in caskets behind a storefront window, under a sign that said MURDERED IN THE STREETS OF TOMBSTONE. They were later buried at Boot Hill.

Holliday and the Earp brothers were put on trial for murder. The trial lasted a month, and the defendants were declared innocent. That didn't keep friends of the cowboys from seeking revenge. Two months after the gunfight, Marshal Virgil Earp was ambushed in the dark by unseen assailants in front of the Cosmopolitan Hotel. His left arm was shattered forever. He tried to console his wife by saying, "Never mind. I've got one arm left to hug you with."[3]

✴❨ 2 ❩✴

THE GUNFIGHTER

Gunfighters in the Wild West were a self-confident, flashy breed. They didn't try to avoid trouble—they *looked* for it. They considered gunfighting to be an art, like painting or writing poetry.

There were two distinct classes of gunfighters: outlaws and lawmen. They often squared off against one another—outlaws on the side of wrong, lawmen on the side of right.

Reputation

Whether they were good or bad at heart, all gunfighters had one thing in common. They were feared and famous. Gunfighters seemed to command a certain respect from the average townsfolk. Everyone knew of men like Tulsa Jack Blake, Bully Brooks, Dynamite Dick

Clifton, Flat Nose Curry, and Turkey Creek Jack Johnson.

Most gunfighters enjoyed their reputation. It made them feel powerful when men would clear out of the way as they rode through town on their horses, or walked through a saloon to the bar. When these gunfighters would get drunk, they would boast about how many men they had killed, or, even worse, how many they *planned* to kill. Some liked to exaggerate. Wild Bill Hickok, for instance, once bragged to a reporter that he had killed over one hundred men. This is known to be a wild lie.

Not all gunfighters bragged, however. There was one spectacular shoot-out in Newton, Kansas, in 1871; the hero of that story was never found. A pack of cowboys came rushing into a dance hall with guns blazing. Out of nowhere, a thin boy jumped in front of them and fired away, killing four of the cowboys. When the smoke cleared, the boy could not be found. No one knew anything about him, except that his name was Riley, and that he was dying of some disease.

The Quick Draw

Gunfighters knew that if they made one mistake, they wouldn't get a chance to make another, so they spent long hours practicing the art of handling guns. The most common gunfighting technique was that of drawing the six-shooter from the holster. Gunmen tirelessly

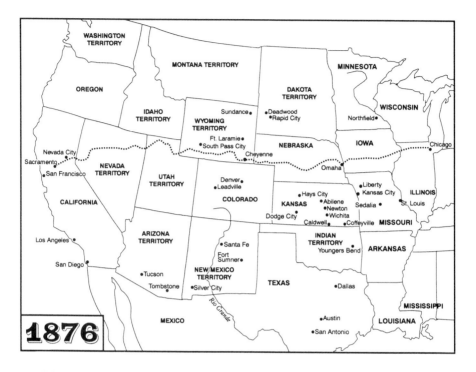

Western America in the 1870s was a jumble of states and territories. Most of the territories were still largely empty of white settlers. It was easy for outlaws to hide from the law in the wide-open spaces.

rehearsed the movement—reach and draw, reach and draw—until they could draw, cock, and fire all in one smooth lightning-quick movement.

The Gunfight

The legendary gunfight in the Wild West was the duel. In reality, it wasn't a common practice, simply because most shootings ended swiftly, often with one cowardly man shooting another in the back. The duel was thought to be the fairest way to settle a dispute, though. Opponents would stand back-to-back with guns drawn. They would carefully step a set number of paces away from each other. Then they would turn and fire. Sometimes they wouldn't even bother with the steps. They would just meet in the street a distance away and stare each other down, each waiting for the other to reach for his gun. Either way, the man left standing would live to see another day—probably not for long, though. Gunfighting was a hazardous affair.

There were two sure places in the Wild West where you could find gunfighters—saloons and banks. Fights

Bullet holes pierce the walls and windows of this bank in Coffeyville, Kansas. Robbing a bank was the ultimate challenge for an outlaw.

usually erupted in saloons when men drank too much liquor. These brawls often involved punches, kicks, and sometimes a few thrown bottles, or broken chairs—not much more.

Bank Robbing

Banks were a different story. Outlaws robbed banks with guns; shoot-outs resulted. People were killed, and only the best gunmen survived.

Some gunfighters considered it a challenge to rob a bank. Henry Starr, one of the last outlaws to do his robbing while seated on a horse, told a reporter for the *St. Louis Globe* about the thrill of bank robbery.

> It isn't only the lure of money that takes a man into outlawry, there's the thrill of dashing into a town after an all-night ride, guns blazing. From every window across the street rifles and shotguns are spitting lead at you. The boys who had gone into the bank come running out with a grain sack bulging with loot. It's time to leave. One of your boys is down, stretched out in the dust. You realize there is nothing you can do for him. You vault into the saddle and roar out of town, guns bucking. You think of the boy you left lying back there in the dust. It's tough, but you realize that it may be you the next time.[1]

⋙ 3 ⋘

THE OUTLAWS

Some men weren't satisfied with earning a decent living. They imagined having riches and fame. They figured that being quick on the draw gave them the right to take anything they wanted. So they became outlaws.

Outlaws came from all sorts of backgrounds. Some had been on the dodge from the law ever since they were children. Others learned to handle a gun fighting in the Civil War. Some had been upstanding individuals in the community before turning bad. A few even wised up later in life to become decent citizens, or even lawmen. A few were wealthy, but most were poor. A few were along in years when they turned bad, but most were just youths when they began a life of crime. A few were educated, but most were quite ignorant.

Nearly all outlaws shared one common trait—they did not obey the law of mutual respect. They thought, wrongly, that they were more important than anyone else. Their friends were afraid to challenge them for fear of getting hurt or killed. So they rode along, shooting and hurting people, until they wound up in prison—or dead.

The Cruelty of Outlaws

The behavior of some of the outlaws who roamed the Wild West was downright cruel. Bill Longley once shot a man to death in a camp because he thought the man was looking at him while he tried to sleep. John Wesley Hardin is said to have killed forty-four men in ten years. In one of his first killings, when he was fifteen years old,

Gunslinger Bill Longley is apprehended by Sheriff Mast and Bill Burrows. Longley once killed a man because he thought the man was watching him sleep.

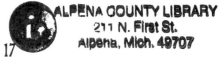

Hardin drilled three bullets through his cousin after an argument. Who could forget the notorious Cole Younger, who eventually joined the James Gang? Legend has it that during the Civil War, Cole tested a rifle by firing it into the backs of several Union prisoners tied together and stacked against a tree. He wanted to see how many bodies one bullet would go through.

Clay Allison

One of the most notorious outlaws was sharpshooter Clay Allison. He was considered insane by many, though no one dared tell him so to his face. Among Allison's favorite hobbies was riding stark naked up and down the street on his white horse, then inviting flabbergasted citizens to the saloon for a drink.

Allison once broke into a jail with a mob and lynched an accused murderer. Allison then cut off the dead man's head and placed it on a pole in a saloon.

Allison often drew his gun and shot at anything or anybody. One evening, he was shooting the lights out of a saloon in New Mexico when the town marshal approached him. The marshal asked Allison kindly to stop, and Allison wheeled around and shot him. Another time, when Allison and his brother entered a dance hall, the marshal asked them to remove their guns. Allison drilled bullets through the marshal's heart.

Even when Allison wasn't shooting people, he was wreaking other kinds of havoc. A dentist once drilled the wrong tooth in Allison's mouth. Allison went off angrily to another dentist to have the procedure done right. He later returned to the first dentist. The outlaw grabbed the dentist, pinned him to the chair, and yanked out three of the dentist's teeth—without administering an anesthetic.

John King Fisher

Many outlaws were ruthless. A Texan named John King Fisher once shot a man through the head, apparently for no reason. People joked that Fisher wanted to see if the bullet would bounce off the man's bald head. Fisher was arrested for this crime, and for several others, through the course of his evil young life, but he was never held in jail for long. Sometimes the prosecution could find no witnesses, usually because citizens were afraid to testify against Fisher. Sometimes Fisher was released from jail early because of overcrowding.

Shortly after being released from the Texas state penitentiary in 1871, Fisher teamed up with a group of Mexican rustlers. While splitting up the money following the sale of stolen cattle, Fisher shot three of the Mexicans dead. He then took control of the rustling operation and was reputed to have killed several more men while selling stolen Texas cattle across the border in Mexico.

Fisher befriended another notorious gunfighter, Ben Thompson, who had many enemies in San Antonio,

Texas. When the two outlaws entered that town one day, Fisher's friend was gunned down—and so was Fisher. He was found dead with thirteen bullets in him.

Billy the Kid

Perhaps the most famous outlaw of all was Henry McCarty. You might know him better as Billy the Kid. Billy had his first brush with the law in the town of Silver City, New Mexico, when he was fifteen. Billy took part in a practical joke by hiding a bundle of clothes from a Chinese laundryman. He was caught and tossed in the local jail to learn a lesson. After sitting still for two days, Billy could stand it no longer; he escaped by climbing up the chimney. He didn't stop running until he reached Arizona. Billy had become a fugitive.

Billy the Kid was known throughout the West for his daring and impossible escapes from the law.

Billy eventually was befriended by a wealthy New Mexico cattleman and banker named John Tunstall. Billy had no parents, and he thought of John Tunstall as a father. At the time, rival merchants and ranchers were caught up in a feud known as the Lincoln County War.

When a rival posse showed up one day to steal Tunstall's horses, Tunstall protested. He was immediately shot in the head. Billy was standing nearby when his boss was gunned down. He couldn't believe his eyes. He did not give chase because he was hopelessly outnumbered, but Billy pledged to avenge Tunstall's murder.

He searched for Tunstall's killers with a group that called itself the Regulators. Billy's group found two of the killers in the countryside. The two men surrendered with the promise of being returned to the town of Lincoln alive. On the way back to Lincoln, Billy pulled out his rifle and shot them both dead. Then he gunned down one of the Regulators, who had tried to protect them. A few days later, Billy encountered Sheriff William Brady and his deputies. Shooting from behind a stone wall, Billy killed the sheriff and one of the deputies.

By now, Billy was being tracked all over New Mexico. He became famous for his amazing escapes from the law. One time he was captured and thrown in jail, with iron cuffs around his wrists and feet. He was sentenced to death by hanging. Two weeks before the execution,

This is the grim scene after a feud in Rawlings County, Kansas. When Billy the Kid's friend, John Tunstall, was killed in a feud like this one, Billy vowed to avenge his death.

the Kid somehow managed to kill both guards and break free. There was just no holding Billy the Kid.

On July 13, 1881, time ran out on Billy. Sheriff Pat Garrett rode to Fort Sumner after learning that the Kid was hiding nearby. The sheriff went to the home of an old friend named Pete Maxwell. It was midnight, and Billy was visiting a young Mexican woman in a building on Maxwell's ranch. Sheriff Garrett went into Maxwell's bedroom to wake the rancher. At that moment, Billy walked across the yard to Maxwell's house to get something to eat. When Billy saw a strange horse tied up outside, he went in to see Pete Maxwell. He stepped inside Maxwell's bedroom.

The room was dark, and Billy could not see. He said, "Who are they, Pete?" Sheriff Garrett was sitting on the edge of the bed. Maxwell whispered to the sheriff, "That's him."[1] Billy knew someone else was in the room, and he yelled in Spanish, "Quien es? Quien es?" ("Who is it? Who is it?")[2]

Right then, Sheriff Garrett jumped up with his pistol and fired a shot at Billy. The bullet pierced his heart. Garrett dived to the floor and shot again. This time he missed, but it didn't matter. Billy fell to the floor, gasping for air. In another minute, Billy the Kid was dead.

Sheriff Pat Garrett killed Billy the Kid, one of the Wild West's most feared outlaws. Twenty-eight years later, Garrett was gunned down himself.

4

THE GANGS

Most outlaws probably realized that they would someday meet their match. Whether it was death in a gunfight by a quicker-drawing foe, or a bullet to the back of the head, outlaws were sure to get it as long as they stayed criminals.

A few outlaws wised up and went straight. Many, however, sought protection by joining forces with other outlaws. The more guns on their side, they figured, the better their chances of shooting their way out of trouble. They would have to split the loot with their partners, but that was better than the alternative—death.

These groups formed by outlaws were called gangs, and among the gangs of the Wild West were some of the most fearsome gunfighters alive.

A favorite target of outlaw gangs was the town bank. It was where most of the citizens' money was kept, and it was usually well guarded. When the robbery was over, a gang's gunfighting work had just begun. Lawmen and citizens alike usually tried to shoot the robbers. If the gang escaped out of town, a posse often was formed to chase after them. The robbers needed great sharpshooting skills, as well as a little luck, to fight off the pursuers.

Gangs weren't satisfied with robbing only banks. They robbed trains, stagecoaches, and ranches, too. Wherever money or horses or cattle could be stolen, gangs usually lurked nearby.

The James Gang

No gang was more notorious than the James Gang, led by Jesse and his brother, Frank. The James Gang rode high for fifteen years, making at least twenty-six big robberies.

It all began for the James Gang on a February afternoon in 1866. A dozen men rode into Liberty, Missouri. They stopped in front of the Clay County Savings Association bank; two of them went inside. One of the men walked up to a bank teller and took out a six-shooter. He demanded all the money in the bank. It was a strange request; an American bank had never been robbed before in broad daylight. The two men hurdled over the counter and pointed their guns at the bank teller. The teller hurried to the vault, opened it, and poured into a sack all the gold, silver coins, and dollar bills the sack

Frank and Jesse James pose with their guns drawn. For fifteen years, the brothers and their gang terrorized the West, robbing banks and trains.

could hold. The two robbers dashed out of the bank with the loot. They mounted their horses, and galloped down the street. A nineteen-year-old college student was on his way to class when he saw the riders coming. He ran to take cover, but it was too late. One robber fired his gun four times at the student, killing him instantly. Later, it was discovered that any one of the four bullets would have been fatal. A posse chased after the gang, but they never did find it. The James Gang made off with about $60,000. The state of Missouri knew it had some real trouble on its hands.

The James Gang began robbing trains, too. Bankers

and train conductors became so desperate that they hired the famous Pinkerton's National Detective Agency to hunt down the James Gang. The detective agency's symbol was an open eye, with the slogan "We never sleep." It is the origin of the term "private eye."

When it was learned that several members of the James Gang were hiding out at a farm near Liberty, Missouri, a Pinkerton agent set out for the farm. The agent's body was found near the farm the next day, shot through the head and heart.[1]

The James Gang finally met its match in Minnesota.

Jesse James and his gang rob a stagecoach.

The townsfolk of Northfield foiled a bank robbery by killing two members of the gang, and wounding several others. A posse hunted down the rest of the gang. Only Jesse and Frank escaped.

The end came for Jesse James on April 3, 1882, at his home in St. Joseph, Missouri. After breakfast, Jesse went into the living room with Charlie and Bob Ford, a pair of brothers who were pretending to help Jesse plan a bank robbery. Really, the Ford brothers were after the reward money that came with capturing or killing Jesse James. Jesse stepped up on a chair to straighten a picture on the wall. Bob quickly drew his pistol and fired a shot into the back of Jesse's head. Jesse collapsed and died instantly. The days of the James Gang finally were over.

Several other gangs tried to imitate the James Gang—and some proved nearly as notorious.

The Daltons

The Dalton brothers—Emmett, Grattan, and Bob—were sharpshooters who grew up near Coffeyville, Kansas. They were cousins of the Youngers. The Dalton Gang gained some attention in 1890 for robbing trains, but they weren't recognized as the ruthless outlaws that their cousins were. This bothered the Dalton brothers; they wanted to be famous and feared. This desire proved to be their downfall.

The Daltons met their doom in their hometown of Coffeyville when they tried to rob two banks at once in

1892. They rode into town disguised in fake beards and mustaches, but townspeople recognized them anyway. They also picked a bad time to pull off the heist. The street in front of the two banks was under repair, and the robbers had to leave their horses a block away and walk to the banks on foot. As the Daltons approached the banks, citizens ran home to get their guns. Merchants passed out firearms to everyone around. The gang managed to seize $20,000 from one of the banks, but they struck out at the second bank when the teller convinced them that the vault had a time lock and could not be opened. The whole town was armed when the Daltons charged out of the banks. A horrendous battle ensued. The gang killed four citizens in the gunfight. All

The gruesome end for the Dalton gang came when they botched a double bank robbery in their hometown, Coffeyville, Kansas.

members of the gang, except Emmett, were also killed. Emmett served fifteen years in prison.

The Doolin Gang

The Doolin Gang was a dastardly band of ten men who killed many people while robbing banks and trains across the Wild West. The gang was organized by Bill Doolin in 1892, and its reign of terror lasted three years, until most of its members had been gunned down.

The Doolin Gang staged carefully planned robberies in an effort to avoid disaster. Still, it seemed that each heist resulted in the loss of one or more members. After a bank in Oklahoma was looted, Crescent Sam Yountis was tracked down by lawmen and shot dead before he could spend any of his $4,500 share of the money. Then a double train holdup resulted in the loss of Arkansas Tom Daugherty. Another train heist led to the death of Tulsa Jack Blake and the expulsion from the gang of Red Buck Waightman, for crazy gunplay. Two more members were killed by gunfire during the holdup of an express office. By then the gang was too small to survive. Bill Doolin returned home to his wife; he died a year later from a lung disease.

The Wild Bunch

One gang that may never have been stopped was the Wild Bunch, led by Butch Cassidy and the Sundance Kid. It is rumored that Butch and Sundance were killed

Butch Cassidy (seated right) and the Sundance Kid (seated left), pose with the Wild Bunch. One of the gang's favorite ways to rob trains was to blow up the safes with dynamite.

in a gun battle with troops in South America. A more popular belief, though, is that Butch died of old age in the United States. Either way, their robberies are legendary.

The Wild Bunch robbed everything—banks, trains, mining camps, and ranches. Butch tried his best not to kill anyone, though. When his gang was pursued by posses, Butch always shot at the horse, not the rider.

Harry "Sundance Kid" Longabaugh was Butch's partner. Harry was nicknamed the Sundance Kid because he served eighteen months in jail when he was a boy for stealing a horse in Sundance, Wyoming. Some say the Sundance Kid was the best sharpshooter in the world.

Butch Cassidy and the Sundance Kid became famous for robbing trains by blowing up their safes with dynamite. They pulled their first heist early on the morning of June 2, 1899. They stopped a train on the Union-Pacific Railroad in Wyoming by flashing a phony warning lantern. Before the conductor knew what was going on, Butch and Sundance disconnected the express car that held the safe. They explained to the guard in the express car that they were going to blow open the car. The stubborn guard refused to leave the express car. So, instead of using two or three sticks of dynamite, they used only one stick, hoping not to injure the guard. The car door blew open, and the guard staggered out, dazed but not hurt. The Wild Bunch used a second stick of dynamite to blow open the safe. Dollar bills flew everywhere. The gang gathered up about $30,000 worth of currency, and then rode off to safety.

They robbed several more trains in the same manner. After many years of such daring tactics, the two outlaws, along with Sundance's sweetheart, Etta Place, fled to South America, where they may have met their fate.

★◀ 5 ▶★

THE LAWMEN

With so many robbers, desperadoes, and gangs on the loose, good citizens were desperate for law and order. They hired men adept with guns to keep the peace. These were the lawmen.

It was the responsibility of the lawman to head off trouble before it began. When shady characters rode into town, the lawman kept an eye on them. Sometimes he asked them to give up their guns. Sometimes he asked them to clear out of town.

Lawmen had a dangerous job. Whether they were marshals, sheriffs, or rangers, they had to stand tall against all enemies. If a gang of sharpshooters rode into town looking for trouble, a lawman would try to rustle up some help from the citizenry. He would deputize men on the spot and hand them guns. When he couldn't find help, he would have to face the gang alone. It was a good thing, then, that some of the best gunfighters in the Wild West were the men who wore the lawman's badge.

Wild Bill Hickok

Perhaps the most celebrated lawman ever was James Butler "Wild Bill" Hickok. Hickok happened to be in Hays City, Kansas, when citizens there were demanding law and order. George A. Custer, a lieutenant colonel at nearby Fort Hays and a Civil War hero, knew of

George Ruffner, sheriff of Yavapai County, Arizona, takes a break in his office. Tough lawmen were needed to keep desperate thieves and rustlers under control.

Hickok's exploits as an army scout. Custer recommended his friend Hickok for the job. The citizens knew of Hickok's reputation, but they decided to take a chance anyway, and they appointed him town marshal. The longhaired Hickok took an instant liking to being on the right side of the law. In a saloon, he killed two men who foolishly drew their pistols on him. He killed a third man—who happened to be his archenemy—when the man tried to outshoot him.

Wild Bill left Hays City after a skirmish in another saloon with members of the U.S. Seventh Cavalry. There is debate over exactly what happened. One version has it that Wild Bill was standing with his back to a group of approaching cavalrymen when suddenly he drew both his six-shooters, firing one over his shoulder and the other to his side, killing two men. Friends smuggled him aboard the next train out of town. When asked later why he fled Hays City, Hickok replied, "I couldn't fight the whole Seventh Cavalry."[1]

Hickok later surfaced in Abilene, Kansas, where he was named marshal. Hickok was a gambler, and he spent most of his time at the poker table. Anyone who needed the town marshal would go to the Alamo Bar, where Hickok played cards.

Wild Bill went too far with his gunplay one day when he fired a barrage of shots into a group of squabbling drunks, killing one of them, and a policeman as well. Hickok resigned immediately, and for a few years he became a drifter. He was killed five years later when a man sneaked up behind him at a poker table and shot him in the back of the head.

Henry Brown

Other towns were having trouble finding and keeping reliable lawmen. In Caldwell, Kansas, three different town marshals were gunned down within one year. Citizens were desperate. One day, a short, blue-eyed man named Henry Brown rode into Caldwell, packing two six-shooters and a Winchester rifle. Henry went to the mayor's office to ask for a lawman's job. "All right," the mayor was reported to have said. "It's your funeral."[2] Henry was named assistant marshal. No one realized Henry Brown was one of the most famous desperadoes of the Southwest. He did such a good job keeping the peace that he was promoted to head marshal within six months. He demonstrated his shooting skills when he killed a man resisting arrest, and when he killed a gambler who tried to outshoot him. Henry's deputy was a big Texan named Ben Wheeler. Together they walked down the streets of Caldwell, toting their guns in the name of law and order.

Henry did not drink, gamble, or smoke. He represented the good, clean image of a lawman. The citizens of Caldwell presented him with a gift of appreciation—a shiny, new Winchester rifle. Henry married a town girl and bought a house. Then, without warning, Henry turned outlaw again. He rode out of town with Ben Wheeler, and they met two more men on the trail. The four men rode to a small town, where they tried to rob a bank. They shot and killed the bank teller, wounded the president, and were soon being chased out of town by a posse. They were cornered in a canyon, captured, and hauled back to town, where they were thrown in jail. That night, an angry mob broke into the jail, over-powered the sheriff, and charged after Henry and his group. Henry made a run for it, and was riddled with

Without warning, marshal Henry Brown of Caldwell, Kansas, (second from left) turned outlaw. He was shot fleeing from a mob of angry townsfolk, and his accomplices were hanged that same day.

Dodge City, Kansas, was a wild frontier town, but rowdy cowboys and gunslingers were no match for town marshals Bat Masterson and Wyatt Earp.

bullets. He died instantly. The other three men were dragged to the edge of town, and were hanged from a tree. The citizens of Caldwell were stunned and saddened.

Ben Thompson

Ben Thompson was marshal of Austin, Texas. He policed his town with the same kind of grit as did Henry Brown in Caldwell. Thompson was a celebrated gunfighter who fought for the Confederate Army in the Civil War, and for Emperor Maximilian's forces in Mexico. Bat Masterson, another lawman, wrote that Ben was "the most dangerous killer in the Old West."[3]

Thompson admitted to killing at least thirty-two men. His presence in Austin made rowdies think twice about causing trouble. Ben would sometimes get drunk and shoot out the street lamps. The citizens of Austin seemed to put up with this behavior. They were happy to have such a fearsome gunfighter looking out for them.

Bat Masterson

Bat Masterson also was appreciated while serving as a lawman in Kansas. One terrible night, he was attacked in a saloon by a group of soldiers and was shot in the hip. Bat would have been killed that night, but Ben Thompson came to his rescue. He challenged the soldiers with his six-shooters. For the rest of his life, Bat walked with the aid of a cane.

Bat served as a deputy marshal in Dodge City with his friend Wyatt Earp. Bat later became sheriff of Ford County, Kansas. He was a quick shooter with deadeye aim, but he seldom used his guns. Most times, Bat took care of trouble by whacking the troublemakers with his cane.

As feared as some lawmen were on the frontier, there never seemed to be enough of them to keep the peace. There were just too many gunslingers on the loose.

⫷◀ 6 ▶⫸
THE END OF
THE GUNFIGHTER

Although the legends don't say so, the life of the gunfighter was usually quite lonely. Gunfighters were always on the move, forever searching for something bigger and better. Most never found what they were looking for. Instead, their lives were almost always cut short by the very tool of their trade—the gun.

Gunfighters in the Wild West lived in fear of dying without their boots on. Many did, and early in life. Few gunslingers lived past their thirties. Many other gunfighters simply disappeared without a trace.

The Taming of the West

Towns grew, and the wide open Wild West became more populous. Citizens insisted on law and order. More lawmen were hired to keep the peace, making it more difficult for desperadoes to shoot their way out of trouble. The mere presence of peace officers made outlaws think twice about causing trouble.

Using modern technology rather than guns made tracking outlaws easier. With the telegraph and later the telephone, lawmen informed one another of the whereabouts of dangerous gunslingers. Loading their horses onto trains, peace officers and posses could speed ahead in the direction that the outlaws were fleeing. The posses would greet the outlaws at their final destination. The lawmen would use the horses for the last miles of the

A man caught stealing a horse lies dead on a lonely dirt road. Many lawmen took pictures of dead outlaws to discourage others from turning to the wrong side of the law.

By 1902, Bat Masterson had had enough of the West. He moved to New York and became a sportswriter and boxing promoter. He died in 1921.

chase. If the chase ended in a deadly gunfight, photographs were taken of the outlaws who were gunned down. It was thought that a picture of a man riddled with bullet holes would prevent future gunfights.

Captured murderers were usually sentenced to death. Public hangings were held in town squares to further discourage would-be outlaws. A double hanging of murderers in Leadville, Colorado, for instance, drew a crowd of ten thousand citizens. The townsfolk hoped that children who witnessed a man hanging from a rope might be less inclined to become bank robbers or murderers.

Fade-out

Eventually this violent breed of men began to fade from society. By the turn of the century, gunslingers galloping into town with guns blazing were a rare sight. The most hardened criminals committed crimes until they were either killed or jailed. Many lawmen were killed in the line of duty.

Those lawmen and outlaws who did survive the dangers of living by their guns eventually hung them up. Some got ordinary jobs, some turned bad, and some, like Wyatt Earp, never really settled down. Until his death in 1929 at the age of eighty, Earp dreamed of finding a big mining stake.

Earp's friend Bat Masterson gave up his lawman's badge, moved to New York, and became a sportswriter. He died, aged sixty-eight, at his desk in the *Morning Telegraph* newspaper office.

Not only lawmen lived on to old age. Emmet Dalton survived the disastrous 1892 Coffyville bank robbery. After serving a fifteen year sentence, he went straight. In 1920, Emmett moved to Los Angeles, where he wrote movie scripts and appeared in a few movies. He died in 1937.

❖❶ NOTES BY CHAPTER ❶❖

Chapter 1
1. Casey Tefertiller, "Wyatt Earp's Last Stand," *San Francisco Examiner* (October 17, 1993), pp. 14–19.
2. Paul Trachtman, *The Gunfighters* (Alexandria, Va.: Time-Life Books, 1974), p. 27.
3. Ibid. p. 34.

Chapter 2
1. Harry Sinclair Drago, *The Legend Makers* (Cornwall, N.Y.: Cornwall Press, Inc., 1975), p. vi.

Chapter 3
1. Paul Trachtman, *The Gunfighters* (Alexandria, Va.: Time-Life Books, 1974), p. 190.
2. Jay Robert Nash, *Encyclopedia of Western Lawmen & Outlaws* (New York: Paragon House, 1989), p. 44.

Chapter 4
1. Paul Trachtman, *The Gunfighters* (Alexandria, Va.: Time-Life Books, 1974), p. 68.

Chapter 5
1. Harry Sinclair Drago, *The Legend Makers* (Cornwall, N.Y.: Cornwall Press, Inc., 1975), p. 26.
2. Paul Trachtman, *The Gunfighters* (Alexandria, Va.: Time-Life Books, 1974), p. 110.
3. W. B. (Bat) Masterson, *Famous Gun Fighters of the Western Frontier* (Monroe, Wash.: Weatherford Press, 1982), p. 38.

⇥◀ GLOSSARY ▶⇤

anesthetic—A painkiller given by doctors and dentists to patients having surgery.

buckshot—Lead bullets fired from a shotgun.

cavalry—A group of army men mounted on horses.

deputize—To make an ordinary person an officer of the law for a short time. In the Wild West, lawmen sometimes needed extra help from citizens to fight outlaws.

desperadoes—Violent, ruthless criminals.

duel—A type of gunfight in which opponents stand back to back, walk a certain number of steps apart, and then turn and fire.

heist—An armed robbery.

marshal—The head lawman of a town.

posse—A group of people who travel together for some common purpose, usually to capture criminals trying to escape.

rustlers—Cattle thieves.

saloons—Places where people could play cards and drink whiskey in the frontier towns of the Wild West.

sheriff—In the Wild West, the chief law officer of a county.

shotgun—A type of gun that is fired from the shoulder.

six-shooter—A revolver with chambers for six bullets.

telegraph—A system of wires that made it possible for people to send messages across long distances.

territories—Regions of the United States owned by the government, but not officially states.

⇥◉ FURTHER READING ◐⇤

Green, Carl R. and William R. Sanford. *Billy the Kid*. [*Outlaws and Lawmen of the Wild West* series] Springfield, N.J.: Enslow Publishers, 1992.

Holbrook, Stewart Hall. *Wyatt Earp, U.S. Marshal*. New York: Random House, 1956.

Marsh, Carole. *Kansas Bandits, Bushwackers, Outlaws, Crooks, Devils, Ghosts, Desperadoes, Rogues, Heroes, and Other Assorted and Sundry Characters*. Atlanta, Ga.: Gallopade Publishing Group, 1990.

O'Neal, Bill. *Encyclopedia Of Western Gunfighters*. Normon, Okla.: University of Oklahoma Press, 1979.

Stiles, T.J. *Jesse James*. New York: Chelsea House Publishers, 1994.

Trachtman, Paul. *The Gunfighters*. Alexandria, Va.: Time-Life Books, 1974.

Yancey, Diane. *Desperadoes and Dynamite: Train Robbery in the United States*. New York: Franklin Watts, 1991.

✦ INDEX ✦

Johnson, Jack, 11

L

lawmen, 33–39, 40–41
Leadville, Colorado, 42
Liberty, Missouri, 25–27
Lincoln, New Mexico, 21
Lincoln County War, 21
Longabaugh, Harry
        (Sundance Kid),
        30-32
Longley, Bill, 17
Los Angeles, 43

M

Masterson, Bat, 39, 43
Maxwell, Pete, 22–23
McCarty, Henry (Billy the
        Kid), 20-23
McLaury, Frank, 5–10
McLaury, Tom, 5–10

N

Newton, Kansas, 12
Northfield, Minnesota,
        27–28

O

O.K. Corral, 8–10
outlaws, 16–23,

P

Pinkerton's National
        Detective Agency, 27
Place, Etta, 32

posses, 37, 41–42

Q

quick draw, 12–13

S

St. Joseph, Missouri, 28
St. Louis Globe, 15
San Antonio, Texas, 19
Silver City, New Mexico, 20
South America, 31, 32
stagecoach robbing, 25,
Starr, Henry, 15
Sundance, Wyoming, 32
Sundance Kid. *See*
        Longabaugh, Harry.

T

Thompson, Ben, 19–20,
        38–39
Tombstone, Arizona, 5–10
train robbing, 25–27, 30–32
Tunstall, John, 21

U

Union-Pacific Railroad, 32
U.S. Seventh Calvary, 35

W

Waightman, Red Buck, 30

Y

Younger, Cole, 18
Yountis, Crescent Sam, 30